Reflections of Portland, Maine

By Frederic Thompson, Publisher
Photographs by Dennis Griggs
Published by Congress Square Publishing

Library of Congress Catalog Card Number: 85-72159

ISBN: 9611320-1-9

Book published and distributed by Congress Square Publishing

Book design by Annette Langley-Hulst, Fit To Print, Portland, Maine

Printed by Ilte, Turin, Italy

Color Separations by Graphic Sales, Danielson, Connecticut

Typography: Serif & Sans, Inc., Boston, Massachusetts

CONGRESS SQUARE PUBLISHING

Acknowledgements

This book would not have been possible without the aid and encouragement of a few individuals and organizations.

Key among them is Annette Langley-Hulst of Fit To Print who, with calm grace and perseverance, designed this book.

Another is John Hagenstein, who engineered this book through the printing process. His firm—Graphic Sales of Danielson, Connecticut—did the color separations, paying special attention to making this a masterful publication. They are true professionals and a joy to work with.

Special credit should be given to Ilte of Turin, Italy, printers of this book. They are master craftsmen and, as you can see, perfectionists in fine printing quality.

Frederic Thompson,
Dennis Griggs

Foreword

Portland is alive with history and with the future-in-the-making. It bustles with busy urban streets reflected in the windows of modern office buildings. It embraces the stillness of an island cloaked in snow. It contains ancient cobble streets and a bright modern art museum. It is a unique and colorful tapestry infused with the spirit of an enthusiastic people.

Where did Portland begin? It began centuries ago at the edge of the harbor with a handful of fishermen and their families. It grew from an outpost to village to bustling trading port to modern urban center. Its history is heaped up in layers, with each era showing through here and there like the cobblestones poking out under the edges of the asphalt streets. ▶

Portland is resilient. The city has rebuilt time and again, after total destruction in the French and Indian Wars and the Revolutionary War and again after the Great Fire of 1866. Now the same spirit has fostered an economic and cultural renaissance after a long seige of depression. A spirit of renovation and renewal pervades the city.

Portland has no simple definition. It is a complex fabric in which you can find threads of past and present, of exquisite and mundane, of familiar and rare, all woven together. You can feel the varied textures. You can sense the whole cloth as a collection of scenes and isolated details. This volume brings you a kaleidoscope of images which capture for you a beautiful and artistic impression of Portland's rich tapestry.

Pamela Plumb

Reflections of Portland, Maine

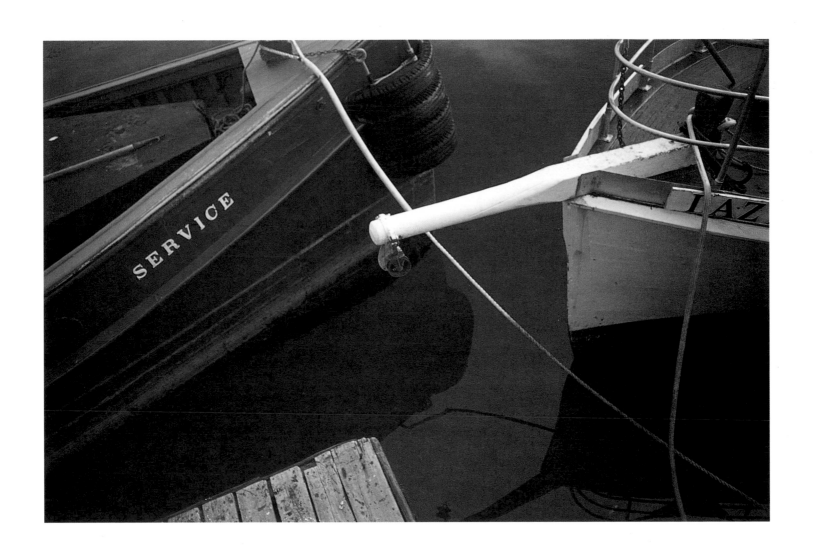

I first met photographer Dennis Griggs on a Rotary International cultural exchange program to Manchester, England, in the spring of 1984. During our trip he shot 100 rolls of film. When I returned to Portland and saw Dennis' slide presentation of our journey, he had reduced the whole visit to 80 images. It was then that I realized it was not how many photographs he had taken, but how well he had chosen those slides. His presentation of Manchester, England was a masterpiece.

I had been at Dennis' side throughout most of the trip, but after viewing his photographs I could not help but wonder if we had been to the same place.

I believe Dennis has done it again. After working on this project for over a year, he has captured the essence of Portland, Maine. Portlanders and visitors alike see hundreds of different images of this beautiful city each day.

But it's the ability to see Portland from a slightly different perspective, a slightly different view, that makes his photographs something special.

I know that you will never look at Portland the same way after seeing this book; never take the beauty of this city for granted; never overlook the simple features that make this one of the finest cities in the world in which to live.

Frederic Thompson

I'm not a native of Maine. Like many people who live in Maine, I can claim no local ancestry. Luck (and the Navy) brought me to the Brunswick area in 1973.

My years of traveling to and from Portland have taught me a great deal about the city. It still amazes me that Portland remains a pleasant thirty-five minutes down 95, a relaxing option to my crazy life in Topsham.

This is a book about Portland— glimpses of a wonderful city are suspended on these pages. When I started this project, I was pretty confident that my knowledge of the city was going to be invaluable.

After the first few months it was evident to me that I was testing new ground, and that Portland had a mind of its own. The two of us were going to make peace with one another, each in our own way. This city offered me a challenge. Finally, the time seemed right and this portrait of Portland emerged.

The directions taken, the sequence of the images and their layout have all been part of a creative process. Two people have been involved with this creative process. One is Fred Thompson, the publisher of the book, an ardent Portlander. Fred personifies the spirit that keeps Portland alive.

The quality of this book reflects the efforts of Annette Langley-Hulst, the designer. From the beginning, she has been a joy to work with. Annette: my thanks.

When I was growing up around the San Francisco Bay area, "The City" was San Francisco. It had everything: the place was a full course meal and I was the guy studying the best part of the menu.

Today, "The City" is Portland, no less a full course meal, offering me all a growing spirit could want.

Dennis Griggs

I'm looking out my window over Congress Square where two of Portland's four mounted policemen have met in their patrolling and stopped for a chat in front of our new art museum.

We experimented with cops on horses a few summers ago, decided it was an idea whose time had come again. Horses are more efficient for in-town patrolling than police cars. And taken on the whole they smell better. Feel better, too. Ever try to pat a police car? Horses are also much more efficient than cars for crowd control. If Portland ever gets a crowd, we're ready.

In over 200 years Portland's had only two traffic jams. The first happened in 1963 when then-President Johnson came to town running for re-election. What was surprising was most people thought we didn't have enough Democrats in Maine to create a traffic jam. But the times are a-changing.

The second occurred when Joan Benoit returned to her hometown following winning the women's marathon at the 1984 Summer Olympics. What a parade we had. It took Joan longer getting from one end of Congress Street to the other riding in the back of a convertible than it did to run the 26 miles and 385 yards at Los Angeles.

On the subject of traffic jams and their causes, we don't have rush hour. We call them "meander minutes."

The other day I slowed the car while turning a corner to allow a pedestrian to get through the crosswalk. Halfway she turned, looked at me and said, "Thank you."

This is a great place to be.

Lew Colby

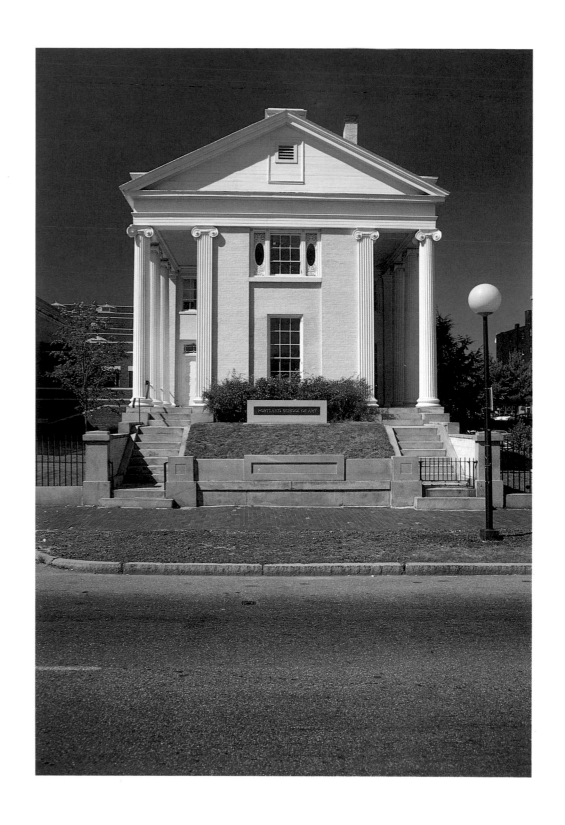

A port is a window on the world through its ships, planes, cars, and trucks that enter and leave daily. Two poets have caught this flavor from different perspectives:

"I remember the black wharves and the ships.
And Spanish sailors with bearded lips.
And the beauty and mystery of the ships.
And the magic of the sea."

Henry Wadsworth Longfellow
from "My Lost Youth"

"A port is a marvelous relaxation for the mind, fatigued by the stress of life. The exposé of the sky, the ever changing shapes of the clouds, the variety of colors of the ocean, the flashing of the lighthouse. All are a marvelous exact prism to stimulate the visual senses without tiring them. The slender shapes of the ships with their intricate rigging to which the swells of the waves and harmonious oscillations serve to imprint on the mind a taste of the rhythm and beauty of it all. And besides, there is a kind of mysterious and aristocratic pleasure for one who has neither the curiosity nor the ambition as he lies on the grass or sits on the breakwater watching the comings and goings of those who still have the wish, the strength and the courage to sail forth whether for pleasure or for business."

Charles Baudelaire
from "Le Port"

"Extol our esplanades" should be the watchword for our public officials and departments of Recreation and Public Works, to increase opportunities for enjoyment of Portland's splendid vistas. Portland's unique port makes the finest city site on the East Coast.

Our port is home to the Western Promenade's unparalleled sunsets and swooping planes, Shailor School's People's Park, and Back Bay's birds, joggers, and stream of cars. We can sit and look through any one of these windows to watch the world go by, knowing that for us Portlanders, there is no need to follow.

Dr. Philip P. Thompson, Jr.

They shouldn't be orange. That "most people like the lights" of the fountain in Deering Oaks doesn't make them beautiful. Portland was born and thrives on natural things.

It is a small complaint to have about a city as glorious as ours, but I hate those lights. I don't hate them as much as the power station in Portland Harbor, or the architecture of the high rise apartment buildings on the Eastern Prom, or the mall built on the ruins of Union Station. But those are big mistakes, hard to rectify. You learn to live with big mistakes.

We've got an electric spirit in Portland that may account for the special light here. And the fabric of the city—its bricks, its harbor, its people—may account for that spirit.

Portland is too good for those orange lights.

Rob Elowitch

This handsome volume, *Reflections of Portland, Maine,* is the culmination of more than a century old tradition of celebrating the city through pictorial publications.

In 1859, on the eve of the Civil War, historian William Willis produced the community's first guide book featuring wood engravings of local landmarks and scenery. After the war, as Portland began to flourish as a tourist mecca, John Neal contributed *Portland Illustrated* in 1874, which was quickly followed by Edward Elwell's *Portland and Vicinity* in 1876.

By the 1890s, wood engravings gave way to black and white photographs in a host of picture books designed for the quarter of a million visitors who came by water and by rail each year. A typical example of the period, Chisholm Brothers' *Portland, Maine and What I Saw There,* enjoyed sixteen printings between 1903 and 1927.

With the economic and social changes of the Great Depression, the presses ceased to produce these invaluable pictorial essays, as though the face of the city had lost its pride and no longer wished to be mirrored.

The last twenty-five years have witnessed an ever increasing return to the prosperity of the 19*th* century, and with it a new awareness of Portland's inherent beauty and value, both natural and man-made. This renewal of faith in the destiny of Portland has manifested itself in many ways. Nowhere is this spirit more appropriately expressed than in the color pages of *Reflections of Portland, Maine.* The presses are rolling once more in celebration of the city.

Earle Shettleworth